Just for Lau

SECRETLY TREASURED JOKES ABOUT PIRATES

Julia Garstecki

BLACK RABBIT BOOKS

Hi Jinx is published by Black Rabbit Books
P.O. Box 227, Mankato, Minnesota, 56002.
www.blackrabbitbooks.com
Copyright © 2022 Black Rabbit Books

Marysa Storm, editor; Michael Sellner, designer
and photo researcher

Library of Congress Cataloging-in-Publication Data
Names: Garstecki, Julia, author.
Title: Secretly treasured jokes about pirates /
by Julia Garstecki.
Description: Mankato, Minnesota : Black Rabbit Books, [2022]
Series: Hi jinx. Just for laughs | Includes bibliographical
references and index. | Audience: Ages: 8-12 |
Audience: Grades: 4-6 | Summary: "Through an engaging
design that brings the jokes to life with fun facts and critical
thinking questions, Secretly Treasured Jokes about Pirates will
have readers laughing and learning"– Provided by publisher.
Identifiers: LCCN 2020016546 (print) | LCCN 2020016547
(ebook) | ISBN 9781623107062 (hardcover) |
ISBN 9781644665619 (paperback) | ISBN 9781623107123 (ebook)
Subjects: LCSH: Pirates–Juvenile humor. | Pirates–Juvenile literature.
Classification: LCC PN6231.P53 G37 2022 (print) | LCC PN6231.P53
(ebook) | DDC 818/.602-dc23
LC record available at https://lccn.loc.gov/2020016546
LC ebook record available at https://lccn.loc.gov/2020016547

Image Credits

Alamy: Matthew Cole, 7; Dreamstime: Aridha Prassetya,
13; Luliia Kolesnikova, 5; Shutterstock: anfisa focusova,
4; Anton Gemini, 15; Artbyinez, 3; Artpaper, 18; Azuzl,
12; Blue Ring Media, Cover, 9; Christos Georghiou, 3, 17,
19; Davide Quaroni, 18; designer_an, 17; deymos, 10–11;
Donnay Style, 8; Dualororua, 6, 15; Dusan Pavlic, 1, 16;
GB_Art, 15; GraphicsRF.com, 21; hermandesign2015,
6; HitToon, 12; Igor Zakowski, 7; Jibon, 14; kaisorn, 6;
Katerina Davidenko, Cover; klyaksun, 7; Liudmyla Kulias,
4; Maciej Es, 17; Macrovector, 17, 20; Memo Angeles,
Cover, 5, 6, 7, 8, 9, 10, 15, 17, 23; Oleksii.1994, 15;
okili77, 8; Pasko Maksim, 7, 14, 23, 24; picoStudio, 9,
16; Pitju, 18, 21; Refluo, 10–11, 23; Ron Dale, 5, 6, 12, 16,
20; Tatiana Gulyaeva, 17; Teguh Mujiono, 14; Tueris, 9;
Yayayoyo, 11, 17, 23; YUCALORA, 17

CONTENTS

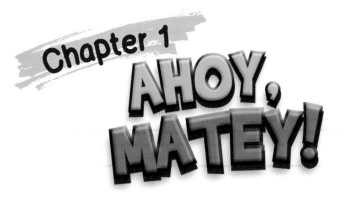

Chapter 1

AHOY, MATEY!

Ahoy! Are ye ready for some pirate jokes? Put on yer eye patch and grab a matey. If ye ever get **marooned** on a **desert** island ye'll be glad ye read this book. It'll keep ye laughin' fer days!

Chapter 2
LIFE ON A PIRATE SHIP

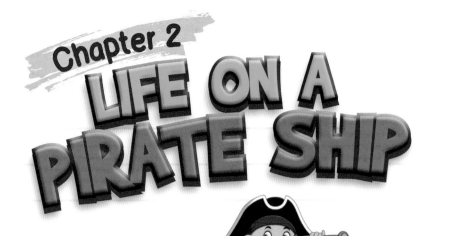

Who steers the ship
when the captain
studies the map?
the co-pirate

What happened when
Captain Bluebeard fell
into the Red Sea?
He got marooned.

What vegetables
are pirates afraid of?
leeks

Why won't a
pirate learn the
entire alphabet?
They love to stay at C.

What's a pirate's
favorite cookie?
Ships Ahoy!

Why did the pirate put
a belt on a pumpkin?
She wanted it to be a squashbuckler.

What do you call a
pirate who skips class?

Captain Hooky

What's a pirate's favorite kind of fish?

a swordfish

A pirate and a sailor were sharing stories.

The sailor pointed to the pirate's peg leg and asked, "How did you get that?"

The pirate said, "Aye, I wrestled a shark and lost me leg."

The sailor pointed to the pirate's hook and asked, "How did you get that?"

The pirate said, "Aye, I fought Blackbeard's crew and lost me hand."

The sailor pointed to the pirate's eye patch and asked, "How did you get that?"

The pirate said, "Aye, a bird flew over me and pooped in me eye. It was me first day with the hook."

Chapter 3
PIRATE EXPENSES

How much does it cost for
pirates to pierce their ears?

a buccaneer

Why was the pirate
ship so cheap?
It was on sail.

How much did the pirate
pay for her peg leg?
an arm and a leg

There might really be pirate treasure in
Davy Jones' locker. Davy Jones' locker is
another name for the bottom of the ocean.

Where do student pirates

put their valuables?

Davy Jones' locker

What did the pirate buy
at the Apple store?

an ipatch and an ayephone

Why did the pirate cross the road?

To get to the second hand shop.

Chapter 4
PIRATE PASTIMES

What's a pirate's best
basketball move?

*a **hook shot***

Why are pirates bad at cards?

They're always standing on the deck.

What's a pirate's favorite movie?

Booty and the Beast

What's a pirate's favorite exercise?

the plank

Why did the pirate take a vacation?

He needed some aarrgh and aarrrgh.

What did one pirate say
to the other during a
game of hide-and-seek?

"I sea you!"

Why are pirates
the best boxers?
*They have a great
right hook.*

Chapter 5

Get in on the Hi Jinx

Talking like a pirate is super fun. So is sailing the seas. If that interests you, you could become a ship's captain someday. You could guide a fancy cruise liner or huge cargo ship. Captains need the help of crews. **Engineers**, **stewards**, and cooks all work together. Working on a ship is a great way to see the world and live an adventure. No peg leg or parrot required.

STEWARD

ENGINEER

COOK

Take It One Step More

1. Pick your favorite joke from the book. What makes it so funny? Write a similar joke.

2. Do you think you would have liked life as a pirate? Do some research to find out.

3. Pick a joke from this book that didn't make you laugh. How could you improve it?

GLOSSARY

booty (BOO-tee)—goods taken from an enemy in war or by robbery

buccaneer (buhk-uh-NEER)—a pirate

desert (DEZ-ert)—a place with very few or no people

engineer (en-juh-NEER)—someone who takes care of a ship's engine

hook shot (HOOK SHOT)—a shot in basketball made usually while standing sideways to the basket by swinging the ball up in an arc with the far hand

leek (LEEK)—a vegetable that has leaves and a thick white base

maroon (muh-ROON)—to abandon in a place that is difficult to escape from

steward (STOO-erd)—a person whose job is to serve meals and take care of passengers on a train, airplane, or ship

BOOKS

Hoena, Blake. *Blackbeard: Captain of the Queen Anne's Revenge.* Pirate Tales. Minneapolis: Bellwether Media, Inc., 2021.

Loh-Hagan, Virginia. *Pirates vs. Ninjas.* Battle Royale: Lethal Warriors. Ann Arbor, MI: Cherry Lake Publishing, 2020.

Terp, Gail. *Pirates.* History's Warriors. Mankato, MN: Black Rabbit Books, 2020.

WEBSITES

Arrrr, Did You Know? 10 Fun Pirates Facts and Myths
www.nassauparadiseisland.com/arrr-did-you-know-10-fun-pirate-facts-and-myths

Corny Pirate Jokes and Pirate Puns
www.rd.com/funny-stuff/pirate-jokes-pirate-puns/

Pirate Facts for Kids
www.dkfindout.com/us/history/pirates/

INDEX